The Sober Church

Study Guide Companion

Table of Contents

Study Guide Description

This guide is designed to serve as a companion to The Sober Church, guiding individuals and faith communities into a deeper understanding of wholeness—both personally and corporately.

The Sober Church invites the people of God to look beyond surface-level expressions of faith and examine what it truly means to be whole as believers and as the Church. Too often, church traditions place heavy emphasis on doctrine, etiquette, emotionally stirring messages, and polished performances within weekly services. While these elements may inspire and encourage, they do not automatically lead to transformation.

Many congregations experience altar calls that do not alter lives and messages that feel powerful yet fail to produce lasting change. As a result, people often walk away from the church the same way they came—broken, bruised, or disillusioned—having encountered the performance of faith without fully experiencing the transforming power of God's presence.

This comprehensive study guide is not designed to condemn these experiences or traditions. Rather, it is a call to go beyond—beyond rituals, religious culture, images, masks, and spiritual bypassing that have left wounds in our souls and fractures in our faith. It challenges individuals and the Body of Christ to press deeper, confronting what has hindered us from being truly free to trust God fully and to live the abundant life He has designed for His children.

The Sober Church forces us to look honestly at the wounds, trauma—both within and outside of the church—and negative experiences that continue to shape our spiritual lives and create barriers to true connection and communion with God. Too often, we serve through pain when we should be sitting and getting healed. We preach through our wounds and fears, which leads to fractures in our faith and hypocrisy that often scatters the flock.

The culture within many churches unintentionally breeds conformity and alienation rather than honoring the uniqueness of God's design and nature. The people of God are often influenced to look like one another because "it's right," it's tradition, or it's etiquette—without stopping to ask the critical question: Is God in it?

Unaddressed wounds and trauma have a way of infiltrating our mental and emotional health, prompting God's people to build walls and defensive structures that block true deliverance, intimacy, and connection with Him. Over time, these defenses replace vulnerability, authenticity, and trust.

Through The Sober Church, readers are guided to identify the areas of their lives that have robbed them of genuine encounters with God. This guide creates intentional space for reflection, truth-telling, healing, and restoration. It also challenges spiritual leaders to examine the cultures within their churches and make a renewed commitment to seek God for authentic transformation.

The experience within this guide is designed for believers at all stages of faith and ministry—from the pulpit to the back door. Whether leader or layperson, this journey invites participants to lay down performance and allow God's presence to bring real and lasting change.

God ordained the Church, and this work is not intended to diminish or pervert what He has called sacred. Instead, it redirects our focus away from elevating the created and back to the Creator, calling God's people to prioritize His presence over performance and relationship over ritual.

Ultimately, this study guide is an invitation to sobriety—spiritual clarity that leads to healing, freedom, and a restored faith rooted in truth, humility, and wholeness.

A Letter from the Author

I am so excited that you have decided to join this journey toward sober living. This work was birthed from a deep belief that the heart of God is to see His people walk in complete wholeness.

I believe the Church is a powerful and sacred space—one designed for like-minded people to grow in faith, deepen fellowship, and live fruitful, purpose-filled lives. At its best, the Church nurtures healing, belonging, and transformation.

The threat to this experience, however, is the presence of unresolved wounds, brokenness, and fractures in our faith. These fractures often emerge from trauma, church hurt, and the misuse of doctrine—when teachings meant to sanctify are instead wielded as weapons.

So often, we praise God, visit altars, and even dance through our pain, yet still go home carrying the same scars of yesterday. We declare the Word of God and profess freedom, yet find ourselves continually confronted by unresolved pain. God desires true freedom, not the appearance of it.

This is not always intentional. Over time, we have become accustomed to performative practices that can unintentionally negate the deeper work of the cross. When performance replaces presence, transformation is delayed, and healing remains incomplete.

This journey invites us to pause, reflect, and allow God to address the places within us that have been shaped by pain rather than truth. It is not about condemnation or criticism of the Church, but about restoration—so that faith communities can become spaces where healing is cultivated, freedom is experienced, and wholeness is restored.

Welcome to the journey. May this experience draw you closer to God, deepen your understanding of His heart, and create space for true transformation to unfold.

Facilitator & Leader Introduction

Thank you for your willingness to lead The Sober Church journey. Your decision to facilitate this work reflects courage, humility, and a sincere desire to see God's people healed, restored, and made whole.

This study is not a typical Bible study, small group series, or leadership training. The Sober Church is an invitation into sobriety—spiritual clarity that requires honesty, self-examination, and a posture of openness before God. As a facilitator or leader, you are not being asked to have all the answers, but to model presence, humility, and integrity throughout this process.

This workbook and study are designed to help individuals and faith communities examine how wounds, trauma, unaddressed pain, and religious culture—both inside and outside of the church—have shaped spiritual experiences and, in some cases, hindered true intimacy with God. It invites participants to move beyond performance, ritual, and spiritual bypassing and into authentic transformation through God's presence.

 ## Your Role as a Facilitator

As a facilitator, your role is not to fix, rescue, or correct participants, but to:

- Create safe, grounded, and respectful space
- Encourage truth-telling without judgment
- Allow silence, reflection, and discomfort to do their necessary work
- Lead with compassion, not control
- Remain attentive to both spiritual and emotional dynamics
- Provide scripturally sound wisdom

This journey may surface grief, anger, confusion, resistance, or revelation. These responses are not signs of failure; they are often indicators that God is working beneath the surface. Be mindful not to rush participants toward resolution or spiritual conclusions. Healing is a process, and transformation requires time.

A Word to Spiritual Leaders

If you are a pastor, ministry leader, or spiritual authority, this study also invites you to participate—not merely facilitate. *The Sober Church* calls leaders to examine personal wounds, leadership posture, church culture, and unspoken norms that may unintentionally perpetuate harm, conformity, or silence.

This is not a critique of the Church, nor an attempt to diminish what God has ordained. Rather, it is a call to steward the Church well, ensuring that God's presence is prioritized over performance, people over platforms, and healing over image management.

Important Considerations

- This study may uncover trauma or emotional pain. Leaders should be prepared to offer referrals or additional clinical care/support when needed. This is not to be in the place of therapy.
- Confidentiality is essential. What is shared in this space should remain protected.
- Avoid spiritualizing pain or minimizing lived experiences.
- Honor diversity in expression, processing, and spiritual maturity.
- Be sensitive to the moving and working of the Holy Spirit.

Final Encouragement

Transformation begins with leaders who are willing to be honest before God. As you lead others through *The Sober Church*, may you also encounter God in deeper ways—allowing Him to heal, refine, and renew both you and the communities you serve.

This is sacred work. Lead it with compassion, courage, resilience, and reverence.

Session Norms

1. Confidentiality Is Sacred

What is shared in this space stays in this space. Stories, emotions, and experiences shared by participants are not to be discussed outside the session. Confidentiality builds trust and allows honesty to emerge.

2. Speak From "I," Not "You"

Participants are encouraged to speak from their own lived experiences rather than making generalizations or assumptions about others. This is a space for self-reflection, not correction. Self honesty is key to growth and success. Each participant and facilitator must be willing to face the truth.

3. Honor Perspectives to enable Healthy Dialogue

This session is not a place to rescue, fix, counsel, or spiritually bypass one another. We listen to understand, not to respond. While dialogue and shared reflection are welcome, this is not a space for debate, persuasion, or defending personal perspectives or differences. Our focus is on presence, not performance—on understanding, not winning. Presence is more powerful than advice.

4. Honor the Pace of the Process

Transformation cannot be rushed. Silence, pauses, and moments of discomfort are welcome here. Each participant is responsible for engaging at a pace that feels safe and honest. Participants will be engaged, but also are not required to talk if they are not comfortable.

5. Respect the Differences of others

People will process God, faith, and healing differently. Diversity in spiritual language, emotional expression, and understanding is expected and respected. Uniformity is not the goal—authenticity and healing is.

6. Discomfort Is a Part of the Process

Feeling challenged, exposed, or unsettled does not mean something is wrong. Growth often requires discomfort. However, no one is required to share beyond what feels emotionally or spiritually safe. If it is determined that disclosing or the disclosing of others is too much, please let the leader know as soon as possible.

7. Leaders Participate, Not Perform

Facilitators and leaders are participants in this journey, not experts standing above it. Vulnerability from leadership helps create safety for the group.

8. Honor God's Presence Above All

This is sacred ground. We remain attentive to God's presence, open to conviction, healing, and transformation—without pressure to produce outcomes or appearances.

Closing Commitment

By participating in this session, we commit to showing up with humility, honesty, compassion, and courage—trusting God to do the work only He can do.

Christ Over Culture

This chapter calls believers to examine the ways church culture, traditions, norms, and expectations can unintentionally rival the authority of Christ. It challenges readers to discern whether faith practices are truly rooted in Christ—or shaped more by cultural acceptance, conformity, and performance. At its core, *Christ Over Culture* confronts the tension between what is familiar and what is faithful.

 ## Learning Objectives

By the end of this chapter, participants will:

- ◉ Understand the difference between Christ-centered faith and culture-driven religion
- ◉ Identify cultural norms within the church that may hinder authenticity and healing
- ◉ Reflect on how conformity can replace conviction
- ◉ Begin examining personal and communal practices through the lens of Christ's truth

One of the most pivotal experiences of the Spirit-filled believer is developing an intimate, personal relationship with Jesus Christ—understanding His personhood, the power of the Holy Spirit, and God's divine purpose for their life. While salvation marks the beginning of faith, intimacy with God is the ultimate goal of the believer and is cultivated through personal experience, not merely through what is taught or observed.

God designed the Church to be a place where believers are educated, equipped, and empowered to grow in unity and wholeness. However, church culture—while influential and formative—can at times drift out of alignment with the heart and mind of God. Culture, shaped by language, habits, beliefs, values, traditions, and practices, can be negatively influenced by false doctrine, poor interpretation of Scripture, and the opinions of man. When left unchecked, these influences can create environments that foster division, offense, trauma, and spiritual stagnation rather than growth and maturity.

This chapter examines how traditions—while often intended to provide continuity, belonging, and shared identity—can become rigid, exclusive, or even harmful when conflated with divine mandate. Practices rooted in "what we've always done" can evolve into traumatic traditions that strip faith of God's power and presence, binding believers to rituals devoid of love, freedom, and transformation. Paradoxically, such traditions are often fiercely defended as "God-ordained," leading to alienation, condemnation, and fractured communities.

Christ Over Culture also confronts the misuse of spiritual authority and the distortion of Scripture for control or personal gain. These patterns undermine trust, compromise spiritual integrity, and pollute church culture, ultimately robbing believers of the core essence of God—love. As Scripture reminds us, true knowledge of God is revealed through love expressed and experienced.

This study guide will challenge believers and leaders alike to discern whether their faith practices are rooted in Christ or shaped by culture, optics, and pretense. When appearance replaces authenticity, the power of the Holy Spirit is quenched, and believers mistake ambition or external success for spiritual fruit. True fruitfulness flows from environments—internal and external—that prioritize God's presence, honest reflection, sound doctrine, and loving community.

Ultimately, *Christ Over Culture* calls the Church back to sobriety—placing Christ above tradition, presence above performance, love above control, and truth above comfort—so that believers may walk in freedom, maturity, and genuine communion with God.

Reflection Questions: *As you reflect on the following questions, prayerfully consider Scriptures that support, challenge, or illuminate your responses. Allow the Word of God to guide your insight, bring clarity, and deepen your understanding as you journal or reflect.*

In what ways have you seen church culture shape behavior more than Christ?

_____

_____

_____

_____

_____

_____

_____

Have there been moments when you felt pressure to conform religiously rather than be authentic and/or led by the spirit?

_____

_____

_____

_____

_____

_____

_____

_____

What traditions or expectations have helped your faith—and which may have hindered it?

_____

_____

_____

_____

_____

_____

Where might Christ be asking you to release culture in order to be submitted to the holy spirit more fully?

_____

_____

_____

_____

_____

Where in your life or faith journey have expectations, authority, or "what was best for you" limited your voice, choice, or freedom?

_____

_____

_____

_____

_____

How did this experience shape the way you relate to God, leadership, or community?

_____

_____

_____

_____

_____

Were there moments when fear, compliance, or silence were mistaken for obedience or love?

_____

_____

_____

_____

_____

How do you personally distinguish between honoring tradition and elevating it above Christ?

_____

_____

_____

_____

_____

Group Discussion:

- What does it look like when culture becomes the authority instead of Christ?
- How can performative faith show up in church spaces?
- Why is it sometimes easier to follow culture than Christ?
- How does culture reward appearance while Christ invites transformation?
- What risks come with choosing Christ over cultural comfort?

Activation & Prayer

Take a moment to reflect honestly before God.

- Identify one belief, habit, or practice you have embraced because it is familiar, expected, or culturally accepted rather than Spirit-led.
- Consider where tradition, appearance, or fear of rejection may be competing with obedience to Christ.
- Commit to one intentional shift—placing Christ above comfort, truth above tradition, and presence above performance.

> Prayer: _Father God, We pray that you would strip away what is performative, rigid, or rooted in fear, and restore what is true, living, and led by Your Spirit. Teach us to follow you even when it challenges what is comfortable or familiar. Help us to see you as our standard, our source, and our authority._

_____
_____
_____
_____
_____
_____
_____
_____
_____
_____
_____
_____
_____
_____
_____
_____
_____
_____
_____
_____
_____
_____
_____

Healing the Healer

When the Spirit-filled believer is in need of healing, unprocessed emotions often take precedence—spoken or unspoken—hindering the transformative work of the Holy Spirit. These unresolved wounds can surface as emotional fragility, disproportionate reactions, dissension within church communities, and the projection of personal pain onto others. Though believers and leaders may appear spiritually active and productive, fractures in faith can remain hidden beneath service, prayer, and religious routine.

This chapter explores how wounds, trauma, offense, and disappointment—experienced throughout life and ministry—can quietly bind both believers and leaders, limiting their ability to fully experience the freedom available in Christ. Healing is not a one-time event; as long as we live, we will encounter pain and require ongoing restoration. The call is not to avoid wounds, but to respond to them with humility and intention.

Drawing on the biblical call to sobriety and soundness of mind, this chapter reframes healing as essential to spiritual maturity. True spiritual sobriety allows believers to separate past trauma from present reality, restoring clarity, discernment, and communion with God. Healing may require rest from service, honest reflection, forgiveness, and at times therapeutic support as part of a holistic approach to wellness. When believers and leaders commit to their own healing, they are able to serve from a place of wholeness—fostering healthy, loving, and spiritually grounded communities where God's presence is not quenched, but fully expressed.

 ## Learning Objectives

By the end of this chapter, participants will be able to:

1. Recognize that healing is a continual and compassionate process for both believers and leaders, not a one-time spiritual event.

2. Identify how unresolved wounds, disappointment, and emotional pain can impact faith, leadership posture, relationships, and spiritual clarity.

3. Understand the biblical call to sobriety and soundness of mind as essential to spiritual maturity and ongoing communion with God.

4. Reflect on personal areas of hurt or emotional fragility that may require intentional healing through rest, reflection, forgiveness, or support.

5. Discern how unhealed wounds can silently shape words, decisions, and leadership posture—recognizing that a wounded soul will often wound others, not out of malice, but out of pain that has gone unnamed and unhealed.

6. Explore healthy and holistic pathways to healing that honor the interconnectedness of mind, body, and spirit, cultivating rhythms of care that support wholeness, and clarity in both personal life and ministry.

Reflection Questions: *As you reflect on the following questions, prayerfully consider Scriptures that support, challenge, or illuminate your responses. Allow the Word of God to guide your insight, bring clarity, and deepen your understanding as you journal or reflect.*

Where in your life or ministry have you continued to serve faithfully while quietly carrying unresolved pain?

_____

_____

_____

_____

How have past wounds, disappointments, or trauma shaped the way you relate to God, leadership, or community?

_____

_____

_____

_____

Have there been moments when your reactions, emotions, or responses felt disproportionate to the situation? What might those moments be revealing?

_____

_____

_____

_____

In what ways might unaddressed pain be influencing how you speak to, lead, or respond to others—knowingly or unknowingly?

_____

_____

_____

_____

Where might you be relying on spiritual activity (prayer, service, worship) to cover pain rather than allowing God to heal it?

_____

_____

_____

_____

_____

Are there areas where rest, reflection, forgiveness, or additional support may be necessary for your wholeness?

_____

_____

_____

_____

_____

How do you define spiritual sobriety in your own life? What would it look like to live with greater clarity, soundness of mind, and freedom?

_____

_____

_____

_____

_____

If healing is a journey rather than a moment, what step is God inviting you to take now?

_____

_____

_____

_____

How might your healing impact not only your own faith, but those you are called to love, lead, and serve?

_____

_____

_____

_____

_____

Group Discussion:

- What are some ways spiritual activity (prayer, worship, service) can unintentionally become a substitute for healing rather than a pathway to it?
- What makes it difficult for believers or leaders to admit the need for rest, support, forgiveness, or healing?
- What kind of church culture supports healing rather than hiding, honesty rather than performance?

Activation & Prayer

Healing begins with awareness, but it deepens through intentional response. As you prepare to pray, take a moment to sit quietly and consider what has surfaced for you during this chapter.

Activation:

- Identify one area where you recognize the need for healing—emotionally, spiritually, relationally, or mentally.
- Acknowledge one pattern where pain may have influenced your reactions, leadership, or relationships.
- Name one step God may be inviting you to take in this season (rest, reflection, forgiveness, support, or surrender).

This reflection is not about you being fixed, it is about you yielding to the work of the holy Spirit to bring Wholeness. This is perpetual and not a one time event.

Prayer: *Father God, we ask that you would heal us of every wound and scare and renew the spirit of our minds in Christ Jesus. You said in your word that who the son has set free is free indeed. Help us to be intentional in surrendering daily so that we might be able to experience transformation daily.*

The Spirit Led Soul

To understand the importance of a spirit-led soul, believers must recognize God's intentional design of the spirit, soul, and body to function in alignment. When the Spirit of God leads the soul—shaping our thoughts with truth, governing our emotions, and aligning our will with God's purpose—the believer experiences sobriety, harmony, and wholeness. This alignment is not automatic; it requires surrender, intention, and ongoing renewal.

Though believers are born of the Spirit, many struggle with emotional pain, trauma, conditioning, and traditions that disrupt alignment and create internal obstructions—barriers that hinder spiritual growth and clarity. God's desire is not division between spirit and soul, but unity that restores us to His original plan of wholeness. When misalignment persists, believers may live spiritually active lives while remaining emotionally bound and disconnected from the fullness of God's presence.

This chapter introduces emotional excavation as a vital process for cultivating a spirit-led soul—inviting believers to acknowledge, confront, and uproot hidden wounds, distorted beliefs, and defensive structures that compete with God's truth. Through intimacy with Christ, courageous identification of pain, intentional instruction, and commitment to transformation, believers are empowered to dismantle strongholds and renew the spirit of their minds.

A spirit-led soul is not achieved through performance, denial, or spiritual bypassing, but through honest surrender and alignment with the Holy Spirit. As believers learn to allow God's Spirit to lead their inner lives, they begin to experience clarity, soundness of mind, and freedom—walking in the fullness of who God created them to be.

 Learning Objectives

1. Understand God's intentional design of the spirit, soul, and body to function in alignment for wholeness and spiritual maturity.

2. Recognize the role of the Holy Spirit in leading the soul—shaping thoughts, guiding emotions, and aligning the will with God's purpose.

3. Identify areas of misalignment caused by trauma, conditioning, traditions, or unprocessed emotional pain that hinder spiritual clarity and growth.

4. Acknowledge how emotional suppression, denial, or spiritual bypassing can create internal obstructions that block God's transforming work.

5. Explore the process of emotional excavation as a pathway to healing, renewal, and spiritual alignment.

6. Embrace a holistic vision of transformation that integrates spiritual, emotional, and relational healing—allowing believers to live from freedom rather than fragmentation.

Reflection Questions: *As you reflect on the following questions, prayerfully consider Scriptures that support, challenge, or illuminate your responses. Allow the Word of God to guide your insight, bring clarity, and deepen your understanding as you journal or reflect.*

In what areas of your life do you sense your soul (thoughts, emotions, or will) leading more than the Spirit of God?

_____

_____

_____

_____

_____

How have past experiences, trauma, training, or traditions shaped the way you think, feel, or respond— possibly creating misalignment within you?

_____

_____

_____

_____

What does a spirit-led soul look like in your daily life right now? Where do you desire greater clarity or peace?

_____

_____

_____

_____

Are there emotions or patterns you tend to suppress, spiritualize, or avoid rather than acknowledge and address with God?

_____

_____

_____

_____

What "defensive structures" have you built to protect yourself from pain, and how might they now be limiting your growth or freedom?

_____

_____

_____

_____

_____

Where might God be inviting you into emotional excavation—to uncover, name, and heal what has been hidden?

_____

_____

_____

_____

_____

How comfortable are you with surrendering control of your thoughts, emotions, and decisions to the leading of the Holy Spirit?

_____

_____

_____

_____

_____

What practices help you stay aligned with God's truth, and which ones may need to be strengthened or reimagined?

_____

_____

_____

_____

_____

What is one intentional step you can take this week to cultivate a more spirit-led, sober, and aligned life?

_____

_____

_____

_____

Group Discussion:

- As a church community, what does it mean to be spirit-led rather than driven by habit, routine, or tradition?
- How can a church tell when it is operating more from emotion, reaction, or culture than from the leading of the Holy Spirit?
- In what ways can misalignment—caused by unaddressed pain, fear, or past experiences—show up in church culture?
- How do defensive patterns (avoiding hard conversations, maintaining appearances, resisting change) impact our ability to grow and remain healthy as a body?
- How can the church create an environment where people feel safe acknowledging weakness, asking for help, and pursuing healing?
- What practices help us stay aligned with God's truth as a community, and which practices may need to be re-examined or renewed?
- How does a spirit-led soul in individual believers contribute to unity, love, and clarity within the entire church?
- As a church, what is one area where we sense God inviting us into greater alignment, healing, or wholeness?

Activation & Prayer

Take a moment to reflect honestly before God. Consider where your thoughts, emotions, or decisions may be leading more than the Spirit of God—both personally and as a church community. Acknowledge any pain, fear, or patterns that may be creating misalignment or limiting spiritual clarity. Commit to one intentional step toward alignment, whether through rest, reflection, forgiveness, accountability, or renewed obedience.

> Prayer: *Father God, We come before You with humble hearts. Where we have allowed emotion, habit, or tradition to lead us more than Your Spirit, forgive us and realign us. Heal what has been wounded, restore what has been fractured, and renew the spirit of our minds in Christ Jesus. Make us sober-minded, sound in spirit, and aligned with Your truth—individually and together—so that our lives and our church reflect Your heart.*

Journaling and Reflection Prompts

Truth and Transformation

True transformation begins when believers recondition their thinking and embrace God as their ultimate defensive structure. As we have already explored, convergence between the Spirit of God, the Word of God, and our will is essential for sober living and spiritual maturity. Convergence occurs when what we know, what we believe, and how we live come together as one. It is the point where spiritual understanding moves into lived transformation—where faith is practiced, not just professed.

Without convergence, believers may read Scripture, experience God's presence, and desire change—yet remain divided internally. With convergence, the believer experiences sober living, spiritual clarity, and wholeness because every part of their being is aligned with God's truth and purpose.

Transformation is activated when the Word of God moves beyond something we read and becomes something we live—shaping our thoughts, emotions, choices, and behaviors.

When the soul—our thoughts, emotions, and will—is in turmoil and competing with the spirit, believers often remain bound by past trauma, distorted thinking, and cycles of self-sabotage. Drawing from both Scripture and clinical insight, this chapter emphasizes that transformation is impossible without truth. Healing requires rejecting false beliefs rooted in pain and replacing them with God's truth, allowing renewal of the mind and restoration of spiritual clarity.

This chapter also addresses the paradoxical nature of faith—holding God's truth even when lived experiences contradict it—and highlights the role of the Holy Spirit in helping believers navigate these tensions. Through intentional self-examination, daily surrender, and renewal of the mind, believers are invited into deeper convergence: the integration of Spirit, Word, soul, and body.

Truth and transformation meet where faith permeates every area of life, producing maturity, integrity, and freedom. As believers allow God's truth to instruct, correct, and train them, they become living reflections of His presence—agents of change both individually and within the church community.

 Learning Objectives

1. Understand the role of truth in activating transformation and sustaining sober living.
2. Recognize the importance of convergence between the Spirit of God, the Word of God, and the believer's will.
3. Identify false beliefs and thought patterns rooted in trauma, pain, or experience that hinder spiritual growth.
4. Apply principles of mind renewal and self-examination to replace distortion with God's truth.
5. Embrace a lifestyle of convergence that integrates faith into daily life, producing maturity, freedom, and integrity.

How do you currently define truth in your life—by God's Word, your experiences, or your emotions?

_____

_____

_____

_____

Where have past trauma, disappointment, or pain shaped beliefs that may be competing with God's truth?

_____

_____

_____

_____

In what ways have you allowed the Word of God to inform your understanding, but not fully transform your thinking or behavior?

_____

_____

_____

_____

How do you recognize when your soul (thoughts, emotions, will) is in conflict with your spirit?

_____

_____

_____

_____

_____

What false narratives about yourself, God, or others might God be inviting you to release in this season?

_____

_____

_____

_____

_____

Have you learned to hold faith and pain, trust and uncertainty, or obedience and discomfort at the same time?

_____

_____

_____

_____

_____

Where do you see a need for greater convergence between the Spirit of God, the Word of God, and your will?

_____

_____

_____

_____

_____

How often do you intentionally examine your attitudes, reactions, and decisions against Scripture rather than against people or culture?

_____

_____

_____

_____

_____

What practices help you renew your mind regularly, and which ones may need to be strengthened or reestablished?

_____

_____

_____

_____

What is one truth from God's Word that you sense He is asking you to not only believe—but to live out more fully?

_____

_____

_____

_____

Group Discussion:

- As a church, what does it look like for us to allow God's truth—not tradition, habit, or preference— to shape how we live and serve?
- How can we tell when we are engaging Scripture for understanding but not fully allowing it to transform us?
- What does it mean for a church to hold God's truth with grace, especially when it challenges comfort or familiarity?
- How can we better support one another in renewing our minds and walking out truth in daily life?
- As a church, what is one area where we sense God inviting us into deeper transformation and alignment with His truth?

Activation & Prayer

Take a moment to reflect honestly before God—both personally and as a community. Identify where you have the knowledge of "truth" but not yet embodied in your life or within the church. Invite the Holy Spirit to reveal areas where alignment between the Spirit, the Word, and the will is needed. Commit to one intentional step toward transformation—whether through self-examination, renewed obedience, repentance, forgiveness, or a change in practice. This is not about perfection, but about posture: a willingness to allow God's truth to shape how we think, live, and serve.

Prayer: *Father God, help us to believe your word, stand on your promises and to allow the word of God to be manifested in our daily choices, thinking patterns, and behaviors. We declare that we are transformed by the renewing of our minds in Christ Jesus.*

Journaling and Reflection Prompts

Church as an Organism

God designed His creation to function in interdependence, not isolation. Just as the human body is made of many parts working together, the Church—the Body of Christ—was created to operate as a living organism, not merely an organization. Spirit-filled believers were never meant to thrive alone; fulfillment and wholeness are found through connection, unity, and love. Love is the essential force that binds the body together.

This chapter invites believers to see themselves as integral parts of God's agenda of wholeness. Each believer has a unique, God-ordained function, and the health of the whole body depends on every part embracing its role and remaining connected. When isolation, comparison, competition, or division take root, the body weakens and the flow of God's power is disrupted.

The chapter also confronts the ladder mentality that can emerge in church culture—where spiritual growth is measured by titles, visibility, or proximity to leadership rather than divine positioning and obedience. This mindset treats the Church as a hierarchy to climb instead of a body to be placed within by God. When ladder thinking replaces spiritual discernment, ambition and self-promotion can overshadow calling, humility, and faithfulness.

Rather than functioning as a rigid hierarchy, the Church is re-centered here as a Spirit-led organism—alive, relational, and responsive to God. While structure and order have their place, they must never suffocate the movement of the Holy Spirit or distort God's design for placement within the body.

The Church is multifaceted in its function: a family where believers belong and are nurtured, a hospital where healing and restoration take place, and an armory where believers are equipped and sent out to fulfill the Great Commission. These expressions do not compete—they converge. Together, they reflect God's design for a unified, healthy, and mobilized body.

Ultimately, this chapter calls the Church back to unity—across differences in background, denomination, and perspective—anchored in love and truth. When believers understand their interconnectedness, reject ladder-driven ambition, and commit to God's agenda of wholeness, the Church becomes a powerful, living witness of God's presence, purpose, and redemptive power in the world.

 ### Learning Objectives

1. Understand the Church as a living organism—interdependent, Spirit-led, and united in Christ—rather than merely an organization.
2. Recognize the power of love, connection, and interdependence as essential to the health and wholeness of the Body of Christ.

3. Identify how isolation, comparison, competition, and division weaken the Church and hinder God's agenda of wholeness.

4. Discern personal and communal roles within the Body of Christ, honoring the uniqueness and function of every member.

5. Differentiate between healthy structure and organizational thinking that can suppress the movement of the Holy Spirit.

6. Embrace the Church's multifaceted identity as family, hospital, and armory—each expression working together for God's purpose.

7. Commit to fostering unity across differences in background, denomination, and perspective, grounded in love and truth.

8. Apply a mindset of interconnectedness that strengthens both individual faith and the collective witness of the Church.

Reflection Questions

Where have you experienced the Church as a place of life and connection—and where has it felt more like an institution than a living body?

_____

_____

_____

_____

Has hurt, disappointment, or misunderstanding ever caused you to withdraw from the Body of Christ? What has that separation cost you—and what has it cost the body?

_____

_____

_____

_____

In what ways might God be calling you to return, reconnect, or re-engage with the body in this season?

_____

_____

_____

_____

Where have comparison, competition, or insecurity tried to distort your understanding of your role within the Church?

_____

_____

_____

_____

_____

Are there places where you have sought position, recognition, or protection rather than purpose and obedience?

_____

_____

_____

_____

_____

Where have you observed a ladder mentality in the Church—ambition, competition, or pursuit of visibility—replacing divine positioning, obedience, and God-ordained function within the Body of Christ?

_____

_____

_____

_____

_____

How has division—whether personal, relational, denominational, or cultural—weakened the witness and power of the Church in your experience?

_____

_____

_____

_____

_____

What would it require for you to fully embrace your God-ordained function without diminishing the function of others?

_____

_____

_____

_____

_____

If the Church truly functioned as a healed organism—family, refuge, and armory—what would need to change in you and around you?

_____

_____

_____

_____

_____

What truth is God revealing that calls you to renew, restore, or recommit to unity?

_____

_____

_____

_____

_____

Group Discussion: This conversation is meant to foster honesty, humility, and healing—not blame or comparison. You are encouraged to speak from personal experience and to listen with grace.

- What stood out to you about the Church being described as an organism rather than an organization?
- How does ladder thinking impact unity, trust, and the health of the Body of Christ?
- What does divine positioning look like in contrast to climbing for recognition or influence?
- In what ways might the Church unintentionally operate more like a business or hierarchy than a Spirit-led organism?
- In what ways has God been challenging the Church to move from hierarchy to harmony?

- How do love, humility, and honor act as prophetic correctives to the fractures we see within the Body of Christ?

Activation & Prayer

Breathe deeply and release the need to compare, compete, strive, or perform. This is a moment of positioning, not productivity.

Invite the Holy Spirit to guide this reflection:

- Ask yourself: What part of the Body has God designed me to function in?
- Reflect honestly: Have I been operating in alignment, or striving for position, recognition, or approval?
- Consider: Where have I withdrawn, disconnected, or isolated because of pain, offense, or disappointment?
- Identify one way God is inviting you to reconnect, realign, or recommit to the Body—not out of obligation, but out of love and obedience.

Prayer: *Father God, teach us to honor every member of the Body—seen and unseen, vocal and quiet, public and hidden. Remove insecurity, jealousy, and envy from our midst, and replace them with humility, trust, and love. Let us function not as competitors, but as co-laborers. We declare that Your Church is a family that nurtures, a hospital that heals, and an armory that equips and sends. Let healing flow where there has been wounding. Let strength rise where there has been weariness. Let unity replace division. Teach us to flourish where You have planted us. May Your Spirit breathe fresh life into this Body. Let love be our connective tissue. Let truth guide our movements. Let wholeness be our testimony.*

_____
_____
_____
_____
_____
_____
_____
_____
_____
_____
_____
_____
_____
_____
_____
_____
_____
_____
_____
_____
_____

God's Agenda Is Wholeness

This chapter teaches that God's desire for His people is wholeness—spirit, soul, and body living in harmony under the leadership of the Holy Spirit. A major pathway to this wholeness is spiritual sobriety: living alert, vigilant, and intentional in one's walk with God. Sober living produces clarity of mind, discernment, and stability, helping believers resist distraction, deception, and cycles that hinder growth. It strengthens endurance, allowing faith to remain steady through trials without surrendering to fear, temptation, or weariness.

The chapter also challenges believers to go beyond altar experiences. While deliverance, prayer, and spiritual gifts can be powerful turning points, they are not substitutes for the daily work of transformation. True change is sustained through ongoing alignment—renewing the mind with the Word, cultivating healthy support through fellowship, and embracing healing resources God provides, including therapy and mental health care when needed. The chapter highlights that spiritual deliverance and clinical care are not enemies; when approached with wisdom and humility, they can work together as part of God's provision for wholeness.

A key emphasis is that wholeness requires maintenance. Breakthroughs must be guarded, nurtured, and filled with truth—because an "empty house" can become vulnerable again (Luke 11:24–26). God's design is not for believers to survive through rituals while remaining internally wounded. Instead, He calls His people into truth-based transformation that changes thoughts, behaviors, and emotional patterns.

Finally, the chapter introduces rest as a holy and necessary component of healing. Rest is framed as stewardship, not weakness—an essential discipline that creates space for renewal, clarity, and divine direction. Restorative and divine rest allow believers to listen to what is happening inside, establish boundaries, recover capacity, and realign with God's rhythm. The chapter concludes with the reminder that sober living stabilizes the believer over time—building self-control, spiritual maturity, and resilience—so God's people can experience the abundant life Christ promised and walk in the fullness of His agenda: wholeness.

 ## Learning Objectives

1. Define spiritual sobriety and explain its role in sustaining clarity, discernment, and stability in the believer's daily walk with God.

2. Distinguish between altar experiences and lasting transformation, identifying the practices required to maintain healing and deliverance.

3. Recognize the intersection of spiritual formation and mental health, understanding how both contribute to God's agenda of wholeness.

4. Identify personal patterns, beliefs, or behaviors that hinder wholeness and contribute to cycles of instability or burnout.
5. Explain the biblical foundation for rest as a sacred and necessary component of healing, renewal, and spiritual maturity.
6. Assess personal capacity and boundaries, recognizing when rest, support, or healing is needed in a given season.
7. Articulate a holistic view of wholeness that integrates spirit, soul, and body in alignment with God's design.
8. Commit to at least one intentional practice that supports sober living, inner healing, and long-term spiritual growth.

Reflection

How would I describe wholeness in my own life right now—where am I aligned, and where am I fragmented?

_____

_____

_____

_____

_____

In what ways am I practicing spiritual sobriety, and where do I notice a lack of clarity, vigilance, or discipline?

_____

_____

_____

_____

_____

Have I ever relied on altar moments or spiritual experiences without doing the ongoing work required for transformation?

_____

_____

_____

_____

_____

How do I typically respond to pain—do I process it, spiritualize it, perform through it, or ignore it?

_____

_____

_____

_____

_____

Where might God be inviting me to pursue healing through both spiritual and practical means (prayer, therapy, rest, community, boundaries)?

_____

_____

_____

_____

_____

What beliefs do I hold about mental health that may need to be surrendered or reframed in light of God's truth?

_____

_____

_____

_____

_____

How do I know when my capacity has been exceeded, and what signals does my body or spirit give me?

_____

_____

_____

_____

What does rest look like in my current season, and why might I resist it?

_____

_____

_____

_____

_____

Have I ever equated constant activity or service with spiritual maturity? What has that cost me?

_____

_____

_____

_____

_____

What boundaries do I need to establish or strengthen to protect my peace and support healing?

_____

_____

_____

_____

What would it mean for me to steward my life as a temple of the Holy Spirit—practically and honestly?

_____

_____

_____

_____

What daily rhythms or practices help me remain sober-minded and grounded in truth?

_____

_____

_____

_____

_____

What is one concrete step God is calling me to take in this season toward greater wholeness?

_____

_____

_____

_____

_____

Group Discussion: This discussion is not intended to condemn the Church or its practices. Rather, it is an opportunity to deepen understanding and to strengthen the sense of wholeness—both personally and communally. Our goal is to reflect honestly, engage with compassion, and explore how God's agenda of wholeness can be more fully experienced in our lives and within the Body of Christ.

- In what ways can church culture unintentionally encourage people to perform through pain rather than heal?
- What are some common misconceptions about mental health within the church, and how might those beliefs hinder wholeness?
- How can the church better support healing by honoring both spiritual practices and mental health care without creating division?
- Why do you think rest is often resisted or undervalued in faith communities?
- How do burnout, overcommitment, or "suffering in silence" show up in ministry and leadership cultures?
- What would it look like for this church or group to become a safe space for honesty, healing, and restoration?

Activation & Prayer

Take a moment to become still. Place your feet firmly on the ground and take a deep breath. As you exhale, release the pressure to perform, fix, or explain. This is a moment of alignment, not effort. Now reflect quietly on the following:

- Ask the Holy Spirit to reveal one area of your life where wholeness has been interrupted— emotionally, spiritually, mentally, relationally, or physically.

- Acknowledge what has been avoided, rushed, spiritualized, or carried in silence.
- Identify one practice God is inviting you to commit to in this season (rest, boundary-setting, therapy, prayer, community, Scripture, or honest reflection).
- Release the belief that healing must happen through effort alone, and receive God's grace for the process.

Prayer: *Father God in the name of Jesus, We submit ourselves wholly unto you. May the God of peace Himself sanctify me through and through making me pure and whole and undamaged, consecrated to Him,set apart for His purpose. I declare that my spirit and soul and body has been complete and found blameless at the coming of our Lord Jesus Christ. Thank you for your unrelenting love and grace that give me wellbeing, a future and an expected end.*

Glossary of Concepts

I. Traumatic Traditions

Traumatic traditions are church practices, beliefs, or cultural norms that were formed in pain, fear, control, or misunderstanding—and have been passed down as "spiritual" despite causing harm to the soul, distorting truth, and hindering wholeness. They look spiritual but leave the soul wounded. In *The Sober Church*, traumatic traditions are not defined by their age or familiarity, but by their impact. Scripture calls the Church to examine all traditions through the lens of love, mercy, truth, and freedom.

They often:

- Spiritualize suffering instead of healing it
- Normalize silence around abuse, trauma, or emotional pain
- Confuse endurance with maturity and pain with holiness
- Reward performance over authenticity
- Use Scripture to control behavior rather than liberate the soul
- Discourage questioning, lament, or emotional honesty

These traditions may have originally developed as survival mechanisms—responses to persecution, scarcity, generational trauma, or cultural pressure. However, when left unexamined, they become vehicles of harm, shaping church culture in ways that fracture faith rather than restore it.

In a traumatic tradition, believers may be taught—explicitly or implicitly—to:

- Serve while wounded
- Pray instead of processing pain
- Forgive without confronting harm
- Obey without understanding
- Submit without safety

Over time, this creates fractures in faith, emotional suppression, spiritual bypassing, and disconnection from God's presence. People may appear faithful, disciplined, and active in ministry while internally remaining bound, fearful, or numb.

In contrast, *The Sober Church* calls for holy examination—a willingness to discern whether traditions produce life or injury, freedom or fear, healing or harm. It does not dishonor the Church or its history; it honors God by returning to His original intent: wholeness, truth, love, and freedom.

Sober faith does not reject tradition—it redeems it by asking:

- Does this practice align with God's heart?
- Does it reflect love, truth, and healing?
- Does it produce freedom and maturity in God's people?

Scriptural Anchor:

Mark 7:8–9 (AMP) "You disregard the commandment of God and cling to human tradition... You are experts at setting aside the commandment of God in order to keep your tradition."

Matthew 9:13 (AMP) The scribes and Pharisees tie up [a]heavy loads [that are hard to bear] and place them on men's shoulders, but they themselves will not lift a finger [to make them lighter].

Isaiah 29:13 (AMP) "These people draw near with their words... but their hearts are far from Me."

Psalm 147:3 (AMP) "He heals the brokenhearted and binds up their wounds."

Fractures in faith are internal breaks or wounds in a believer's trust, belief, or spiritual confidence that occur when painful experiences collide with unprocessed theology, unmet expectations, or unresolved trauma. These fractures do not mean the absence of faith; they indicate faith under strain. Fractures in faith are not the end of belief—they are the place where sober, mature faith is formed.

Fractures often form through:

- Church hurt, spiritual abuse, or leadership failure
- Traumatic life events that contradict what one believed God would do
- Misused Scripture or doctrine that silenced pain rather than healed it
- Repeated disappointment without space for lament, questions, or truth-telling

When faith fractures, believers may still:

- Attend church
- Serve faithfully
- Pray and read Scripture
- Yet internally, they may struggle with:
- Doubt they feel ashamed to name
- Emotional distance from God
- Cynicism, distrust, or guardedness
- A sense of disillusionment masked by religious activity

In *The Sober Church*, fractures in faith are treated not as failures, but as invitations to healing. Just as a fracture in the body requires attention, stabilization, and time to heal, fractures in faith require honesty, truth, compassion, and the restoring work of God's presence.

Left unaddressed, fractures can harden into:

- Spiritual numbness

- Religious performance
- Isolation from community
- Loss of intimacy with God

But when acknowledged and brought into the light, fractures become places where:

- Faith is refined
- Trust is rebuilt
- Theology is healed
- Wholeness is restored

Mark 9:24 (AMP) Immediately the father of the boy cried out [with a desperate, piercing cry], saying, "I do believe; help [me overcome] my unbelief."

Isaiah 42:3 (AMP) "A broken reed He will not break [off] And a dimly burning wick He will not extinguish [He will not harm those who are weak and suffering]; He will faithfully bring forth justice.

Psalm 34:18 (AMP)"The Lord is near to the heartbroken; And He saves those who are crushed in spirit (contrite in heart, truly sorry for their sin).

II. Paradoxical Paradigms

Paradoxical paradigms are spiritual realities in which two seemingly opposing truths coexist under God's sovereignty. They challenge natural logic but deepen faith by requiring believers to trust God beyond what they see, feel, or fully understand.

In the life of a believer, paradoxical paradigms sound like:

- I am hurting, yet I am whole in Christ.
- I am surrendered, yet I am powerful.
- I am weak, yet I am strong.
- I am waiting, yet God is working.
- I am disciplined, yet I am free.

These paradoxes are not contradictions—they are invitations to maturity. They require spiritual sobriety: the ability to hold God's truth even when lived experience feels unresolved or contradictory. Paradoxical paradigms move believers from emotional reactivity to spiritual discernment, from performance to trust.

In church culture, paradoxical paradigms expose tensions such as:

- Order and Spirit-led movement
- Structure and surrender
- Tradition and transformation
- Correction and compassion

When misunderstood, these tensions can lead to confusion, rigidity, or spiritual bypassing. When embraced through the Holy Spirit, they become spaces of growth, humility, and deeper dependence on God.

Paradoxical paradigms teach the believer—and the Church—to live by faith rather than sight, to submit without losing identity, and to trust that God's truth remains steady even when circumstances feel unstable.

Scriptural Base:

2 Corinthians 12:9-10 (AMP) "My grace is sufficient for you... for power is perfected in weakness."

Galatians 2:20 (AMP) "I have been crucified with Christ... the life I now live I live by faith."

Romans 6:22 (AMP) "But now since you have been set free from sin and have become [willing] slaves to God, you have your benefit, resulting in sanctification [being made holy and set apart for God's purpose], and the outcome [of this] is eternal life."

2 Corinthians 5:7 (AMP) "for we walk by faith, not by sight [living our lives in a manner consistent with our confident belief in God's promises]"

III. Convergence (in the context of The Sober Church)

Convergence refers to the intentional alignment and integration of the Spirit of God, the Word of God, and the believer's will so that faith is not compartmentalized but fully embodied in everyday life.

In the context of *The Sober Church*, convergence means:
- God's truth (the Word) shaping how we think and believe
- God's Spirit guiding our discernment, conviction, and direction
- Our will submitting in obedience, not just agreement

Convergence occurs when what we know, what we believe, and how we live come together as one. It is the point where spiritual understanding moves into lived transformation—where faith is practiced, not just professed.

Without convergence, believers may read Scripture, experience God's presence, and desire change—yet remain divided internally. With convergence, the believer experiences sober living, spiritual clarity, and wholeness because every part of their being is aligned with God's truth and purpose.

Simply put: Convergence is where truth, surrender, and transformation meet.

Scriptural Anchor:

1 Thessalonians 5:23 (AMP) "May the God of peace Himself sanctify you through and through [that is, separate you from profane and vulgar things, make you pure and whole and undamaged—consecrated to Him—set apart for His purpose]; and may your spirit and soul and body be kept complete and blameless..."

Romans 12:2 (AMP) "Be transformed and progressively changed [as you mature spiritually] by the renewing of your mind..."

James 1:22 (AMP) "Be doers of the word, not merely hearers who deceive themselves."

2 Timothy 1:7 (AMP) "For God did not give us a spirit of timidity...but [He has given us] a spirit of power and of love and of sound judgment."

IV. Ladder Mentality

Ladder mentality is a way of thinking and operating that treats the Church like a hierarchy to be climbed rather than a body to be positioned within by God. Ladder mentality reflects a worldly approach to influence and advancement, importing hierarchy, ambition, and competition into a spiritual organism. Scripture consistently teaches that God positions His people according to purpose, not preference, and that fulfillment in the Body of Christ comes through obedience, humility, and faithful function—not climbing.

It is characterized by:

- Seeking titles, visibility, or influence as markers of spiritual success
- Measuring growth by rank, platform, or proximity to leadership rather than obedience and fruit
- Competing with others instead of honoring diverse callings
- Viewing advancement as something earned, negotiated, or maneuvered, rather than discerned and appointed by God

In a ladder mentality, the question becomes:
"How do I move up?"
 instead of
"Where has God placed me, and how do I serve faithfully there?"

This mindset often imports organizational ambition into a spiritual organism, replacing divine positioning with human striving. It can distort calling, breed comparison and insecurity, and weaken the health of the Body of Christ by encouraging self-promotion over surrender.

In contrast, divine positioning recognizes that:

- God places each member in the Body as He chooses
- Fulfillment comes from functioning in one's God-ordained role, not climbing toward prominence
- There is no ladder in an organism—only placement, purpose, and interdependence

Scriptural Anchor:

1 Corinthians 12:14–15,18 (AMP) "For the [human] body does not consist of one part, but of many [limbs and organs]. If the foot says, "Because I am not a hand, I am not a part of the body," is it not on the contrary still a part of the body;"But now God has placed and arranged the limbs and organs in the body, each one of them, just as He desired."

Mark 10:42–45 (AMP) "Whoever wishes to become great among you shall be your servant..."

James 3:16 (AMP) "For where jealousy and selfish ambition exist, there is disorder and every evil thing."

Psalm 75:6–7 (AMP) "For not from the east nor from the west... comes exaltation; but God is the Judge."

Ephesians 4:11–12 (AMP)" And [His gifts to the church were varied and] He Himself appointed some as apostles [special messengers, representatives], some as prophets [who speak a new message from God to the people], some as evangelists [who spread the good news of salvation], and some as pastors and teachers [to shepherd and guide and instruct], [and He did this] to fully equip *and* perfect the saints (God's people) for works of service, to build up the body of Christ [the church];"

V. Prophetic Correctives

Prophetic correctives are God-initiated interventions—spoken, revealed, or demonstrated—that lovingly confront misalignment and call people, leaders, or systems back into truth, order, wholeness, and purpose. Correction is not optional—it is a core function of God's Word. It is not condemnation, but divine course correction designed to protect the believer and preserve the integrity of the Church. Sobriety includes discernment and responsiveness to God's correction. They are not condemnations; they are course corrections.

Prophetic correctives function to:
- Expose what is out of alignment with God's heart or design
- Interrupt harmful patterns before they become normalized
- Call repentance, humility, and return without shame
- Restore clarity where confusion has taken root
- Reposition people and communities according to God's intent

In Scripture, prophetic correctives often came when:
- God's people drifted from covenant
- Tradition replaced obedience
- Power replaced humility
- Appearance replaced presence

Prophetic correctives can look like:
- A truth spoken that disrupts comfort but produces freedom
- A conviction of the Holy Spirit that exposes motives
- A seasonal shift where God removes what no longer serves His purpose
- A reframing of identity or calling that realigns function and posture

In the context of The Sober Church, prophetic correctives:
- Confront ladder mentality with divine positioning
- Replace performance with presence
- Restore love as the governing force of the Body
- Call the Church from organization back to organism

Scriptural Anchor:

2 Timothy 3:16–17 (AMP) "All Scripture is God-breathed... useful for teaching, rebuking, correcting, and training in righteousness."

Revelation 3:19 (AMP) "Those whom I love, I rebuke and discipline; so be earnest and repent."

Proverbs 12:1 (AMP) "Whoever loves discipline loves knowledge."

VI. Converging Identities Within the Church

In *The Sober Church*, infirmary, armory, and family are not competing identities—they converge. The infirmary heals, The armory equips, The family sustains. Together, they form a living organism where believers are healed, strengthened, loved, and sent—without ladder mentality, performance culture, or spiritual pretense.

Infirmary (The Church as a Place of Healing)

In the context of *The Sober Church*, the infirmary represents the Church as a sacred space where wounded, weary, and hurting people encounter healing, restoration, and grace. The infirmary does not define believers as permanently broken, but as people in process. It is a place of mercy where God ministers to the whole person—spirit, soul, and body—through His presence, His Word, community, and sometimes professional support.

The infirmary:

- Honors the reality of trauma, church hurt, and emotional pain
- Creates space for honesty, confession, prayer, and restoration
- Rejects performance, shame, and spiritual bypassing
- Allows people to sit, heal, and be tended to before being sent

Scriptural Anchor:

James 5:14–16 (AMP) "Is anyone among you sick? He must call for the elders of the church... and the prayer of faith will restore the one who is sick."

Armory (The Church as a Place of Equipping and Sending)

The armory represents the Church as a place where believers are trained, equipped, and prepared to live out their faith beyond the walls of the church. It emphasizes readiness, authority, and spiritual maturity. An armory is not a place to live—it is a place to prepare and be sent. In the sober church, believers are not entertained or immobilized; they are strengthened, commissioned, and released to represent Christ in the world. Healing without equipping leads to fragility; equipping without healing leads to harm. The sober church holds both in balance.

The armory:

- Equips believers with truth, discernment, and spiritual tools
- Trains believers to engage spiritual opposition with wisdom and faith
- Prepares the Church for mission, service, and spiritual warfare
- Emphasizes deployment, not dependence

Scriptural Anchor:

Ephesians 4:11–13 (AMP) "And He gave some as apostles, some as prophets, some as evangelists, some as pastors and teachers, to fully equip and perfect the saints (God's people) for works of service, to build up the body of Christ, until we all reach oneness in the faith and in the knowledge of the Son of God, growing spiritually to become a mature believer, reaching to the measure of the fullness of Christ."

2 Timothy 3:16–17 (AMP) All Scripture is God-breathed [given by divine inspiration] and is profitable for instruction, for conviction [of sin], for correction [of error and restoration to obedience], for training in righteousness [learning to live in conformity to God's will, both publicly and privately—behaving honorably with personal integrity and moral courage]; so that the [a]man of God may be complete and proficient, outfitted and thoroughly equipped for every good work.

Luke 10:19 (AMP)Listen carefully: I have given you authority [that you now possess] to tread on [a] serpents and scorpions, and [the ability to exercise authority] over all the power of the enemy (Satan); and nothing will [in any way] harm you.

Family (The Church as a Place of Belonging and Identity)

The family represents the Church as a relational body rooted in love, belonging, accountability, and shared identity in Christ. It reflects God's design that His people grow best in connection, not isolation. As a family, the Church recognizes that believers are brothers and sisters—not competitors, consumers, or commodities. While families are imperfect and may experience conflict, the goal is reconciliation, maturity, and unity. In the sober church, family does not excuse dysfunction—but it commits to healing it.

The family:

- Provides belonging, not hierarchy
- Cultivates love, honor, and mutual responsibility
- Creates safety for growth, correction, and support
- Values relationship over rank and people over position

Scriptural Anchor:

Ephesians 2:19 (AMP) So then you are no longer strangers and aliens [outsiders without rights of citizenship], but you are fellow citizens with the saints (God's people), and are [members] of God's household,

Romans 12:10 (AMP Be devoted to one another with [authentic] brotherly affection [as members of one family], give preference to one another in honor;

Matthew 12:50 (AMP) For whoever does the will of My Father who is in heaven [by believing in Me, and following Me] is My brother and sister and mother."

VII. Sober Living

Sober living is not about abstaining from substances; it is about spiritual clarity, alertness, and intentional alignment with God. In the biblical sense, sobriety means being awake, vigilant, clear-minded, and self-governed under the leadership of the Holy Spirit.

Sober living invites the believer to live free from distortion—distortion caused by trauma, false beliefs, religious performance, emotional reactivity, or unhealed wounds. It is the posture of a believer whose spirit leads the soul, whose mind is renewed by truth, and whose life reflects integrity rather than impulse.Sober living is not restrictive—it is protective, restorative, and essential to wholeness.

In the framework of The Sober Church, sober living means:

- Seeing clearly — discerning God's voice without the fog of fear, offense, or tradition-driven thinking
- Living intentionally — choosing alignment over autopilot, obedience over performance
- Maintaining what God heals — guarding freedom through daily practices, not just altar moments
- Being emotionally honest — acknowledging pain instead of spiritualizing or suppressing it
- Practicing vigilance — remaining alert to cycles, triggers, and patterns that threaten wholeness

Sober living produces stability. It allows believers to endure trials without losing identity, to serve without self-abandonment, and to love without control or codependence. It is how faith becomes sustainable over time.

Ultimately, sober living is the environment in which wholeness is protected and maturity is formed. It is the disciplined, grace-filled lifestyle that keeps the believer grounded in truth, anchored in love, and responsive to the Spirit—so that transformation is not temporary, but lasting.

Scriptural Anchor:

1 Peter 1:13 (AMP) So prepare your minds for action, be completely sober [in spirit—steadfast, self-disciplined, spiritually and morally alert], fix your hope completely on the grace [of God] that is coming to you when Jesus Christ is revealed.

Titus 2:11–12 (AMP) For the [remarkable, undeserved] grace of God that [a]brings salvation has appeared to all men. 12 It teaches us to reject ungodliness and worldly (immoral) desires, and to live sensible, upright, and godly lives [lives with a purpose that reflect spiritual maturity] in this present age,"

Proverbs 4:23 (AMP) "Watch over your heart with all diligence,For from it flow the springs of life."

I honor you for committing to complete this study guide. Your willingness to engage reflects a desire to grow deeper in communion, commitment, and conviction. This journey requires intentionality, humility, and courage—and your participation matters.

This study guide is designed to invite reflection and purposeful action. The Sober Church was never written to expose the flaws of individuals or to criticize the Body of Christ. Rather, it is a call to return—to the heart and mind of God—as we faithfully walk out our calling, purpose, and assignment on the earth.

Our identity is not rooted in performance, titles, platforms, or ambition. It is anchored in who we are becoming as we reflect the nature, character, and presence of God in the world. This journey is not about perfection, but about posture—the posture of our hearts—and the discipline of daily alignment with truth.

What might happen if we, as a Body, truly aligned ourselves with these truths?

The Sober Church can be used in personal encounters with the Lord to cultivate spiritual maturity and increase sensitivity to His presence. It can also be used corporately to help mobilize the Body of Christ toward collective wholeness, clarity, and maturity. God has divinely ordained fivefold ministry gifts, mental health and medical professionals for the care of the soul and body, and scientific knowledge to support human flourishing. He has also designed nature and the human body with an inherent capacity to heal and restore, reflecting His wisdom and intentional design. These systems—spiritual, psychological, physical, and natural—were never meant to compete, but to work in harmony as part of God's divine plan for wholeness.

Each question, reflection, and discussion—whether engaged individually or in community—creates space to examine and dismantle belief systems, traditions, and practices that may have felt powerful yet quietly diminished the supremacy and efficacy of God's work in His Church. God's design has always included restoration—within the soul, within the body, and within creation itself.

Could it be that God has more for His Church? Could it be that there is still more He desires to reveal? Have fear, control, tradition, or rigid rules limited our openness to His movement?

My prayer is that *The Sober Church* and this Study Guide Supplement serve as tools for deeper maturity, restored connection, and renewed unity within the Body of Christ—so that God's people may walk soberly, love deeply, heal fully, and live aligned with His agenda of wholeness.

Ebony Vaughan

Sources

Primary Source

- Vaughan, E. (2025). The Sober Church. Self-published.
- The Sober Church draws from Scripture, spiritual formation, trauma-informed clinical practice, and systems theory to articulate God's agenda of wholeness—integrating spirit, soul, body, and community.

Scriptural Sources

- The Holy Bible
- Amplified Bible (AMP)
  - New American Standard Bible (NASB)
  - The Message Bible (MSG)
  - Strong, James. *Strong's Exhaustive Concordance of the Bible* – Used for word studies related to sobriety, sound mind, wholeness, and the Body of Christ.
- Vine, W.E. *Vine's Expository Dictionary of New Testament Words* – Used for biblical language clarification and theological meaning.

Mental Health, Trauma, & Psychology

- van der Kolk, Bessel. *The Body Keeps the Score* – Trauma, the nervous system, and embodied healing.
- Ellis, Albert. *Reason and Emotion in Psychotherapy* – Cognitive restructuring and renewal of thinking.
- American Psychiatric Association (APA) – Mental health terminology and best practices.

Rest, Capacity, & Holistic Healing

- Hartley, Laura. *The Art of Restorative Rest* (TEDx Atlanta; articles) – Rest as regulation, healing, and renewal.

Leadership, Systems, & Culture

- Senge, Peter. *The Fifth Discipline* – Living systems vs. organizations (Church as organism framework).

About the Author

Ebony Vaughan is a licensed mental health clinician, author, educator, and faith leader committed to helping individuals, leaders, and communities experience wholeness—spirit, soul, and body. With decades of experience at the intersection of clinical practice, spiritual formation, trauma-informed care, and leadership development, Ebony carries a unique and trusted voice for this generation and the Body of Christ.

She is the Founder and Clinical Director of Nexus Wellness Group, a thriving mental health practice, the Founder and Clinical Facilitator of H.A.V.E.N.—a healing and leadership initiative designed to provide sacred spaces for restoration, reflection, and renewal for ministry and marketplace leaders, helpers, and those carrying emotional and spiritual weight. Through H.A.V.E.N., Ebony facilitates trauma-responsive encounters that integrate faith, mental health, rest, and spiritual formation.

As the visionary behind The Sober Church, Ebony is deeply passionate about dismantling harmful spiritual paradigms, addressing trauma, fractures in faith, and traumatic traditions, and restoring clarity, sobriety, and wholeness to the Church. Her work compassionately challenges performative faith while prophetically calling the Body of Christ back to alignment with the heart and mind of God.

Ebony's approach is both pastoral and prophetic—anchored in Scripture, informed by clinical wisdom, and guided by a deep reverence for God's design for healing, restoration, and maturity. She believes transformation occurs when truth is embodied, not merely taught, and when spiritual formation, emotional health, and intentional living converge.

Through writing, teaching, facilitation, and training, Ebony equips churches, leaders, and communities to cultivate healthy cultures, engage difficult conversations with grace, and walk in sober alignment with God's agenda of wholeness.

Ebony Vaughan is available to facilitate training, workshops, retreats, leadership intensives, and H.A.V.E.N. experiences for churches, ministries, faith-based organizations, and community groups.

If your church or ministry is sensing a call toward deeper alignment, healing, and wholeness, this is an invitation to partner in the work God is doing in this season.

410-773-9706
www.nexuswellnessgroupmd.com

Let us journey together toward wholeness—individually, corporately, and in Christ.

www.ingramcontent.com/pod-product-compliance
Lightning Source LLC
Chambersburg PA
CBHW082250120626
46555CB00009B/3031